SOUTHE
MOROCCO

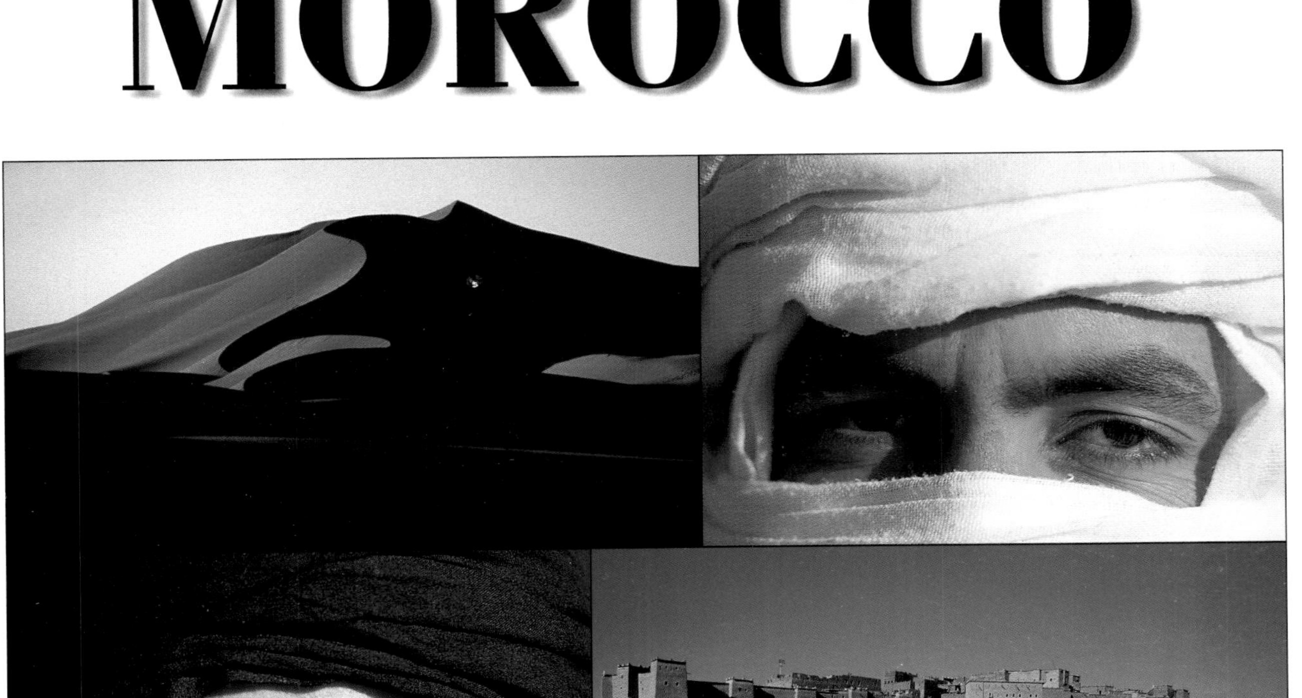

OUARZAZATE – THE DRAA VALLEY –
THE CASBAH ROUTE AND THE DADÈS VALLEY –
THE REGION OF TAFILALET

Distributeur pour le Maroc :
RAIMAGE Sarl.
Angle Rues de Russie et Emsallah
Tél. : 93 42 02, Tanger, Maroc

Editorial management: *Giovanna Magi*
Created and designed by: *Marco Bonechi*
Graphic design, picture research and cover by:
Sonia Gottardo
Layout: *M&M Fotocomposizione*
Editing: *Patrizia Fabbri*
Texts by *Giovanna Magi* and *Patrizia Fabbri* with the collaboration of *Mimoun Hillali.*
Translation: *Eve Leckey*
Drawings: *Stefano Benini*

Printed in Italy by *Centro Stampa Editoriale Bonechi*.

The photographs belong to the archive of *Casa Editrice Bonechi* and were taken by: *Marco Bonechi, Paolo Giambone, Andrea Pistolesi.*
The photographs on pages 54-55 are kindly provided by the *Firm RAIMAGE.*
The photograph on page 57 is kindly provided by *Vivaio Rose Barni, Pistoia.*

The publisher apologizes for any omissions and is willing to make amends with the formal recognition of the author of any photo subsequently identified.

Website: www.bonechi.com

"Morocco is a series of doors that
slowly open as you advance."
Tahar Ben Jalloun

A COUNTRY AND ITS HISTORY

Longer than it is wide, with parallel mountain ranges (the Rif, Anti, High and Grand Atlas) crossing the centre and dividing the country into well-defined zones, Morocco's history, geography and climate have created quite different regions whose coexistence enriches the social, economic and cultural life of the country. Even in ancient times, its position at the centre of important land and shipping routes made Morocco a land of exchanges and encounters. The Phoenicians, Romans, Vandals mingled with the native population of the Libyan Berbers, but it was the Arabs during their wave of conquests in the 7th century who introduced the greatest changes and represent the most powerful influence. The introduction of a new language, a new religion, followed by the establishment of important contacts with the west, and the Islamic conquest of Spain were a vital contribution to the development of Morocco, which gradually extended towards the interior eventually including the great mountain ranges. The distant south also participated as Berber princes departed for Islamic Andalusia where, from the 16th century, the trade with black Africa that had existed since ancient times flourished strongly. Here too the great caravan routes were an essential point of reference for commercial traffic from north to south and across the immense sandy desert. Thus the historic Berber dynasties who had governed the country for centuries (Idriss, Almoravide, Almohade and Merinids) were replaced in the 16th century by Arab dynasties from the south. The Saadians (1525-1656) were powerful merchants, able to control the gold routes, who began a fierce struggle against the occupying Portugese. Later, in the latter part of the

17th century, the Alaouiti family fought to reaffirm the authority of the nation against the expanionist policies of Spain and England. Thus, the great south, the land of casbahs and feudal lords, caravans, nomads and isolated mountain villages, desert and rock, but also of commerce and continual cultural exchanges, was the main contributor to the birth of a modern united state that even in the 20th century however, had to reckon with the schemes of colonial powers (a protectorate existed from 1912 to 1956). And even today, though Morocco is an independent state based on a monarchy and determined to work for development, the south has again assumed a guiding role thanks to its numerous resources and the perfect combination of a magnificent coast open to tourism, and the spectacular interior. Thousands of years of history have created an environment where impeccable gems of architecture and culture are framed in a landscape of rare beauty.

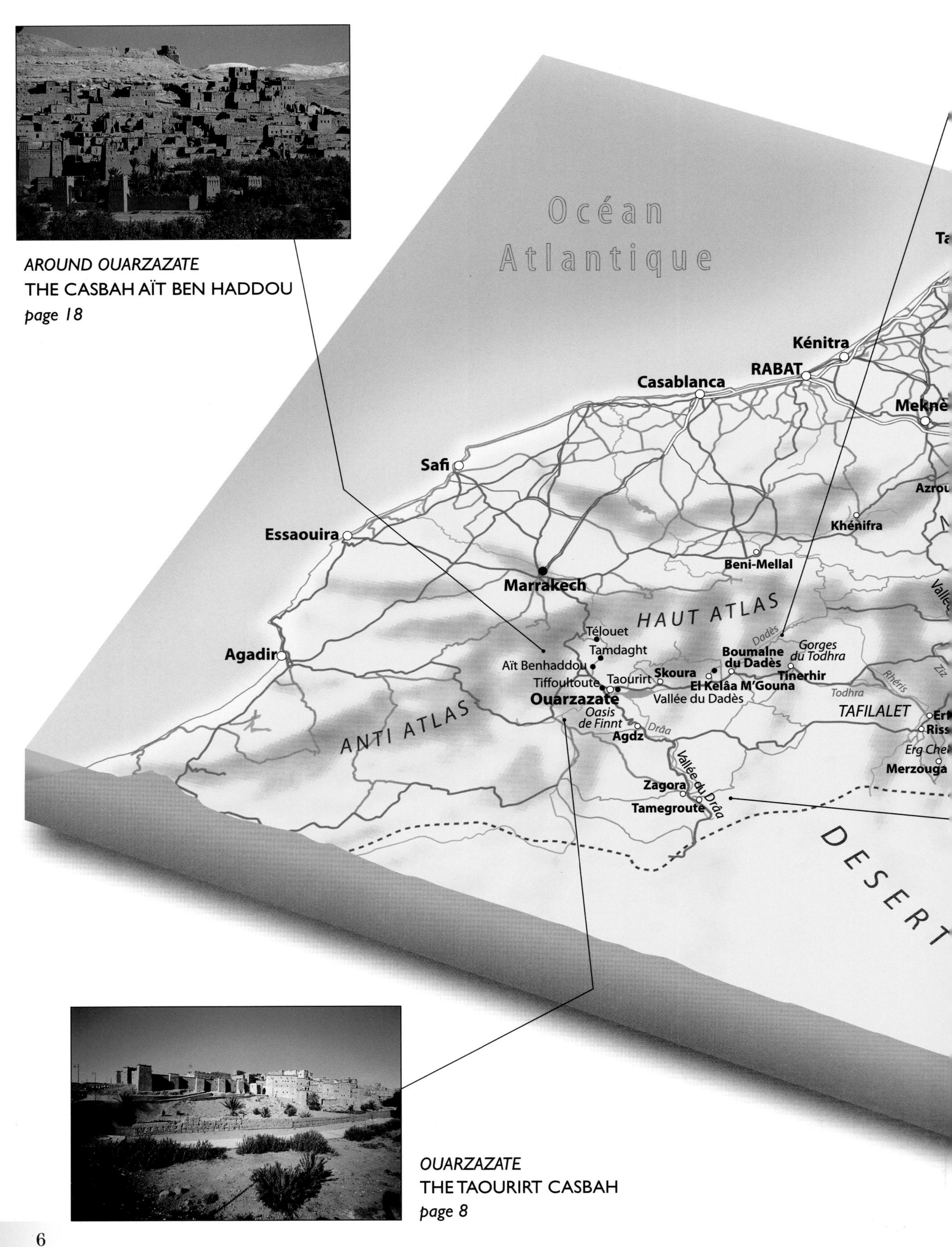

AROUND OUARZAZATE
THE CASBAH AÏT BEN HADDOU
page 18

OUARZAZATE
THE TAOURIRT CASBAH
page 8

THE CASBAH ROUTE
AND THE DADÈS VALLEY
BOUMALNE DU DADÈS
page 48

THE REGION OF TAFILALET
MERZOUGA
page 72

THE DRAA VALLEY
page 32

OUARZAZATE

The name Ouarzazate is derived from the combination of the Berber word *ouar* meaning 'without' and the Arab-Berber *zazate* (plural of *zaza* – 'noise'). 'A place without noise' therefore, and a relaxing tranquility is indeed felt in the silence that reigns in this town, a veritable gateway to the immense desert. Here the trans-Sahara caravans once passed, linking Marrakesh to Timbuktu, to Mali and to the caravanserai of Sahel. Today Ouarzazate, strategic meeting point of the Dadès, Draa, Sous and Marrakech roads, has become one of the main tourist areas of Morocco, particularly suited to those who seek an experience that is peaceful and as far away as possible from the frenetic modern world.

Founded in 1928 as a military garrison, the city later became the administrative centre for the Draa region and developed to take on the role as capital of this large and beautiful area with proud historic traditions, situated between the southern slopes of the Grand Atlas and the northern side of the Anti Atlas mountains. The city remained for long on the fringes of mass tourism and although it has recently undergone rapid urban growth it is still famous for Berber ceramics and especially for the carpets of Ouzguita.

Many bright colours (including those of the famous local ceramics) enhance the streets and imposing ochre-coloured buildings of the village of Ouarzazate.

Eugène Delacroix in Morocco...

In 1831 Louis Philippe of France appointed Charles Edgar de Mornay to organise an expedition accompanying an official French delegation to the Sultan of Morocco. As was often the case at the time, one of the members of the expedition was an artist whose job was to record the journey. On this occasion Eugène Delacroix was chosen. Delecroix departed from Toulon aboard La Perle on 10 January a year later and the emotions and impressions he experienced on the journey changed his personal and artistic development for ever. On his return in July 1832 he recreated an atmosphere of exotic and sensual orientalism in his studio in Paris. Today the paintings, sketches and watercolours illustrating the journey – well over one hundred – are housed in various museums and collections. One of the seven sketchbooks is in the Condé Museum, Chantilly, and three are in the Louvre. A large album of watercolours, known as the 'Morocco Album', reveals most clearly his new sensitivity for colour, contrasting light and vibrant atmosphere.

THE TAOURIRT CASBAH

Approaching from the Boumalen road for Dadès, near to Ouarzazate is the casbah of Taourirt, a name that combines the Arab and Berber languages, meaning “hill fortress” - a structure that is of particular interest both for its fine architecture and its perfect integration into the environmental setting. Originally the residence of the pasha of Marrakesh and a symbol of the feudal period of the lords of Atlas, it consists of buildings that had a mainly military function and developed into a fortified city criss-crossed by numerous alleyways. There is a magnificent view from the terrace of the casbah, across to the mountains and the lake created by the Mansour ed-Dahbi dam, as far as the oases and enchanting Draa Valley.

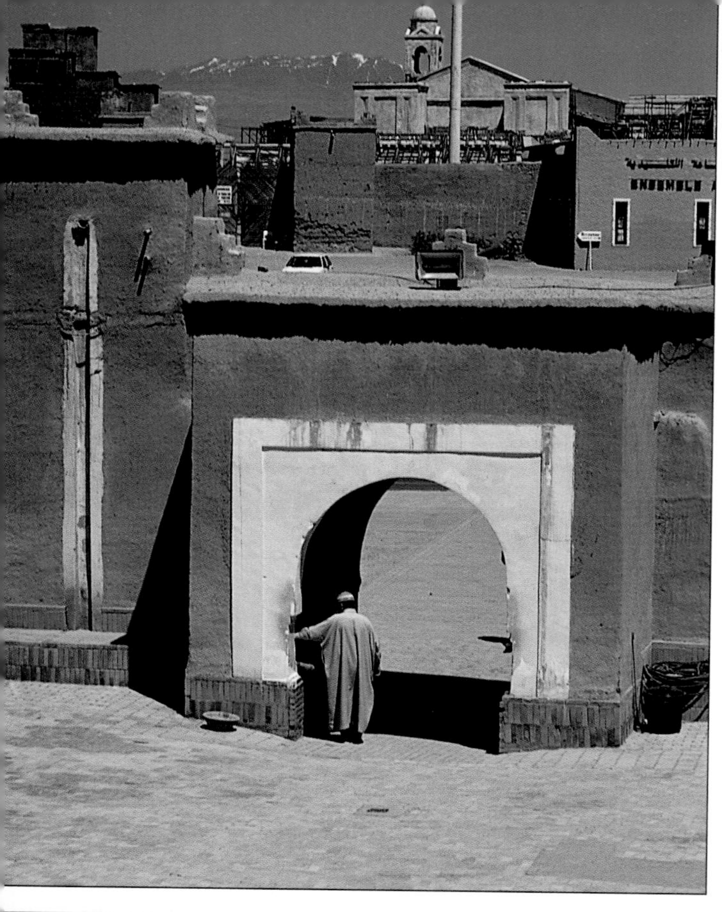

Above all, the natural setting and surroundings offer a panorama of quite magnificent and surprising beauty. The visitor is greatly impressed by three elements: first, the sequence of profoundly contrasting landscapes, all striking in their diversity and extraordinary variety of shades and colours; second, the frequent glimpses of impressive and fascinating casbahs and ksours built from earth. These appear along roads linking a myriad of small towns that have grown in importance due to the presence of a source of water. The third fascinating element is the ring of oases, some of them nestling in the chilly canyons that extend into the depths of the Grand Atlas, some warmer, further to the south, forming small ecosystems that - in a tough but peaceful struggle for survival - defy both the terrible climatic conditions of the desert and man's attempts to change the nature of these special areas.

Fortified gateways, massive walls pierced by narrow windows, imperious deep ochre coloured towers decorated with diamond-shaped motifs and lively little splashes of colour – everything from the granary to the casbah is highly protected and defensive.

11

The craftsmen

Craftsmen are to be seen working in the narrow streets of towns and villages, in the doorways of their houses, in small rooms and beneath the shade of a tent. They sit on a stool, on a low seat, or squat on the floor. In front of them is a work shelf or bench, an improvised surface with a mat on the ground where they sit cross-legged. There is always a teapot and glass of mint tea nearby for a brief pause before starting work once more.

Their materials are clay and wood, metal and wool, leather and stone that they transform into sophisticated, unusual, practical and decorative items – a bowl, rug, necklace or tray.

This is the world of the craftsman, where skills are passed down from one generation to another and the same rythms are repeated day after day. Moroccan craftsmen are the custodians of a genuine cultural

heritage, experts in manual dexterity, they seem to defy the passing of time and the influence of the modern world, remaining untouched by new technologies and industrially produced items.
From the village to the souk where sounds, perfumes and colours mingle, where every stall is unique, attractive, enchanting and captivating.
From one comes the pungent odour of cypress oil and wood, from another the sharp smell of rugs and carpets, while alongside is the glint of silver and further ahead a kaleidoscope of coloured hanks of wool.
Fascinated by the souk, one looses all sense of time, walking for hours to end up at the point of departure, while purchases are won through hard bargaining and thus seem even more valuable.

ATLAS CORPORATION STUDIOS

It is difficult to exaggerate the variety of the Moroccan landscape, the brightness of the light and the magical atmosphere that seems to continually inspire new and original experiences. Thus Morocco has today become one of the favourite film sets of the most famous directors and designers. Scenes from the classic 'Lawrence of Arabia' were filmed in the Todghra Gorge, while the casbah of Aït Ben Haddou was the set for 'Jesus of Nazareth' and 'Tea in the Desert', and the snowy peaks of the Atlas mountains provided the background for 'The Man who would be King'. In 1983, in the wake of this new opportunity, Mohamed Belghmi, a Moroccan businessman already proprietor of the first privately-owned chain of hotels (Salam Hotels), decided to build Morocco's first film studios. Located on the edge of Ouarzazate, they extend over 500 hectares, while the buildings alone cover an area of 150 hectares. Equipped with the most modern film-making techniques, the studios have provided the sets for numerous films: 'The Jewel of the Nile' (1984 with Michael Douglas); an episode of 'Moses' (1995, with Ben Kingsley); 'Kundun' (1996, Martin Scorsese); a new edition of 'Cleopatra' (1998, with Timothy Dalton); 'The Gladiator' (1998-99, Ridley Scott with Russell Crowe); 'Asterix and Cleopatra' (2000, with Gérard Dépardieu).

Aït Ben Haddou

The road form Ouarzazate to Télouet passes through a natural setting of rare beauty with palm groves and verdant areas that owe their existence to the presence of adequate water, including the Ounila wadi. Along the road a series of casbahs can be seen in the distance, their buildings a rich earthy colour. These villages cluster around a strong fortress, an essential stopping point for the caravans travelling this route, but also the centre for small farming communities that, despite the difficulties presented by the terrain, were able to make use of such poor resources for their maintenance. An essential element for existence here are the wadis that flow mainly from the Atlas range, capable, when particular phenomena coincide with a rainfall, of swelling so much that they are difficult to ford and, where there is no bridge, can only be crossed on the back of a dromedary. On the banks of the wadis are small, flourishing oases, filled with lush date palms that not only provide edible fruit but with the shade of their leafy fronds also fulfil the important role of protecting other fruit trees and plots of vegetables and grain from the strength of the sun's rays. In fact, grain, vegetables and fruit are the main produce of the intensive farming practised for centuries on this land by the inhabitants of the ksour, as is evident from the presence in many villages of typical, immense and majestic granary fortresses, known as *ighrem*, in many villages.
Among the numerous casbah and many ksour flanking the long road that crosses the valley, the desert extending on either side, is the magnificent settlement of Aït Ben Haddou, a wonderful fortified village perched on high and a real architectural jewel built of beaten earth. It is, however, precisely this construction material that inevitably represents the greatest weakness of the buildings, being exceptionally subject to attrition by time and especially the weather as is all too easy to imagine.

Views of the fertile areas around Ouarzazate that lie along the bed of the wadi, contrasting with the red earth of the hills in the background and, further in the distance, the snowy heights of the Atlas mountains. Here and there, perched on the heights are small villages, dominated by their characteristic fortified granaries.

CASBAH AÏT BEN HADDOU

This magnificent, earth-built fortified village became one of UNESCO's World Heritage sites in December 1987. Situated on the top of a hill some 40 kilometres to the north-west of Ouarzazate, it is so 'photogenic' that it has been used as the background for some memorable scenes in two film masterpieces – 'Sodom and Gomorrah' and 'Lawrence of Arabia' directed by David Lean.

Tamdaght, though in a poor state of repair, and Tiffoultoute, still impressive and inhabited, are just two of the thousand casbahs situated along these valleys.

Tamdaght

Once the property of the powerful Glaoui family, this impressive casbah, although in a poor state of conservation, still stands majestically dominating a truly magnificent site. Originally the great earth-built villages, the ksour, were built by nomad families who wished to spend a certain period in a fixed location. Although the materials and methods used in their construction are of immense interest, they are also their real weak point. The buildings are exposed to heavy erosion by winds that carry sand with them, and by heavy and violent rain that, with the passing of time and without adequate protection, can reduce these monuments to their original element – the earth.

Tiffoultoute

A few kilometres from Ouarzazate on the Marrakesh road, at a height of 1160 metres, stands the casbah of Tiffoultoute, a historic property of the Glaoui family. Built more than two centuries ago in the characteristic light

Ancient casbahs where storks nest, beautiful oases with plentiful water and images of the unique Berber civilization – the area around Ouarzazate is rich in history and natural splendours.

ochre-coloured hardened clay, it was probably restored at a later date. In the past, its inhabitants represented a threat for Makhzen and Ouarzazate as well as for the surrounding area. Today the casbah boasts a hotel and restaurant and is simply an attraction for passing tourists who wish to enjoy the magnificent view over the valley furrowed out by the Ouarzazate wadi.

Talmassla

The road that leads from Ouarzazate to Tafilelt crosses a network of perennial wadis, an element fundamental for the existence of oases; this water first cuts through the rock of the Atlas Mountains to then gush from canyons and deep gorges. The route is rightly known as the "road of a thousand casbahs" due to the close succession of numerous ksour dominated by their relative casbah, the residence of the village elders, that is also built entirely of earth and stone, and has the impressive, majestic appearance of a defensive fortress. Other casbahs, instead, tower in isolation dominating the immense bleak expanse, but the atmosphere that they seem to provoke in the surrounding environment is always extraordinary. Striking in its evocative solitude is the casbah of Talmassla which is also noted today for a most unusual feature: on the outer walls, now partly damaged by the harsh weather and climate, austere, majestic storks have built their nests.

Finnt Oasis

In Finnt a splendid oasis with 1500 inhabitants and a school, set in an extraordinarily beautiful environment, it is possible to see how the Berber people live today. Finnt is approached from Tinerhir, through the Todghra Gorge, enclosed by mountains and flourshing palm groves, unexpectedly opening out into a green plain which provides a perfect habitat for many species of animals.

THE ATLAS MOUNTAINS

The majestic, jagged "Mountain of Mountains" separates the Atlantic Ocean from the Sahara Desert and extends right up to the Rif massif and over to the coast of the Mediterranean. The chain is made up of a series of mountain ranges, ascending from north-east to south-west: the Anti Atlas, High Atlas, Grand Atlas, Saharan Atlas and Lower Atlas. The High Atlas in particular, *Adrar n'Dern* in Berber, with its glistening snowy peaks soaring above the desert plains, is without doubt the roof of Morocco reaching over 4000 metres in height (the highest summit, Toubkal, is 4167 metres high). At the foot of these cragged peaks lie gentle valleys, filled with flowers in the springtime, dotted with small villages and immense granaries, sweeping down towards the sea where the mountains seem almost to bow down before the Atlantic Ocean. In the warm season, the natural scenery is quite magnificent and visitors discover the unexpected marvels of a country that is on the threshold of the desert.

Soaring snow-capped peaks (an impressive and unexpected sight in an African country surrounded by desert) and immense tree-covered slopes that become thick, flourishing forests as the altitude diminishes, the three ranges of the Atlas mountains form the backbone of Morocco, with deep valleys descending towards the ocean on the western side, while on the east lies the immense Sahara desert.

Andalusian-style decorations and the sturdy, typically Berber buildings are the main features of the casbah of Télouet, an isolated village situated at a height of 2000 metres on the slopes of the Atlas mountains.

Télouet

The highest pass in Morocco is Tizi n'Tichka (2260 metres), meaning the 'passage of pastures', and it marks the border between the western Anti Atlas and the High Atlas. Here, a route winds away from the main Marrakesh–Ouarzazate road, passing close to some interesting salt mines, and leads to the village of Télouet at a height of 2000 metres. This quite splendid casbah is the result of many additions and adaptations first begun in the early 20th century. The grandeur of the typically Berber structures and the magnificent Andalusian style decorations in plaster, carved wood and coloured tiles (an unusual combination of two architectural styles in a casbah huddled in the austere solitude of a mountainous landscape) recall the splendours of the powerful pasha Glaoui, lord of the southern Atlas who died in 1957. The poor state of conservation and the feeling of fragility that

Inside the many spectacular and luxurious buildings that constitute the magnificent casbah of Télouet, two halls in particular have preserved intact their original sumptuous opulence and reveal the typical, traditional bright colours of the Berbers – the harem and the reception hall. At the centre of the ruler's life, these were richly decorated with delicate plasterwork, ceramics and decorations that are clearly of Andalusian origin, including a series of painted ceilings and finely carved doors. Outside are magnificent views and a stupendous panorama can be enjoyed from the heights of Télouet.

today seem to threaten this once powerful fortress are evidence of the increasing and worrying risk of decline and ruin. Such imposing grandeur might appear unusual in an environment that is so wild and unwelcoming – almost lunar in some areas – yet there is a logical explanation that is also evident from the presence of the nearby and interesting Tin Mal mosque (11th century), further west on the road to Taroudant. In fact, for centuries before the advent of the French protectorate, domination of this lofty and strategic chain of mountains was an absolute and fundamental necessity for ensuring control of the plains below.

THE WHITE STORK

Throughout Morocco it is quite normal to see on the roofs of houses, on pylons, on towers, the voluminous nests built by storks. The white stork is a bird quite common to Morocco, with its unmistakeable white plumage tipped with black at the ends of the wings, and with bright red beak and claws. Its wing span can reach as much as 165 centimetres. Male and female collaborate to build a spacious nest and both work together to hatch and raise the chicks. Although the stork does not really have a voice, it does emit a particular, rather intense, noise made by rapidly beating together the two parts of its long beak (which can reach as much as 19 centimetres!). When male and female meet and approach, they throw their heads raised backwards, beating their beaks in unison in a quite unique and unmistakeable greeting.

THE DRAA VALLEY

Also known as the "valley of the thousand casbahs" due to the surprising number of fortified, earth-built settlements located around the oases in particular, the valley of the river Draa (between Ouarzazate and Mhamid) is considered one of the most lovely areas of Morocco. In the past, the Draa was a permanent river with abundant water flowing across some 1200 kilometres before meeting the Atlantic ocean. Its presence is responsible for the numerous palm groves that cover much of this naturally arid valley together with fruit and fig trees and pomegranates. In the upper part of the river's course date palms still grow, indicating the presence of numerous oases, but the waters, which rise not far from Ouarzazate at the foot of Jebel M'Goun, disappear into the sand after less than 300 kilometres of the original route. This is partly due to the el Mansour Eddahbi dam built near to Ouarzazate with the intention of better utilising the waters of the Draa by distributing them more equally to the 50 settlements scattered along the 200 kilometres of the valley. However, the building of the dam was to the detriment of the lower reaches of the Draa Valley where the old river bed, which once wound through fertile land and extensive fields, is now reduced to no more than a dry sandy strip lost in the desert. However, the upper reaches, after a difficult start where the waters struggle to cut a passage through rocky butresses, are striking for the magnificent luxuriance of the surrounding valley, almost like an extremely long oasis (or rather, a circle of irregularly-placed oases). Distinctive features of the numerous Berber villages here are the farms and collective grain stores as well as towers and fortifications built as protection against the incursions of desert nomads. Date palms, acacias, oleanders all flourish, as well as fruit trees and tamerisks, fields of vegetables and cereals (barley and corn), forage and, of course, henna which is a typical product of the valley. It is as if nature had managed to create a corner of paradise in the midst of a desolate and arid desert.

The Draa flows calmly through the valley, passing oases, casbahs and lovely scenery.

Agdz, with its typical red-plastered buildings, stands in the centre of one of the main oases in the Draa Valley. The nearby surroundings are characterised by unusual rock faces that are also of geological interest.

Agdz

At the foot of Jebel Kissane, which flanks the river Draa for a few dozen kilometres, on the road that was constantly travelled by caravans heading south from Ouarzazate during the Middle Ages, is Agdz, a town of typically small houses plastered in red lending them a particularly rural appearance. Agdz is the centre of one of the five main oases in the valley dominating a series of cliffs, literally cut out by the Draa and rather interesting geologically as their unusual stratification lends the mountain a curious striped appearance. A colourful and lively market - distant reminder of its commercial past - is held in the central square of the town where, surrounded by characteristic small shops and cafés, one can buy spices, rock salt, fabrics and metal items decorated in the local style.

THE RIVER DRAA

The river Draa rises in the High Atlas from the confluence of two streams, the Dadès and the Ourazazate, and in ancient times was the longest in Morocco. It might now seem strange, but both Polybius and Pliny in the fifth book of his *Natural History*, mention that originally the 'flumen Darat' was in fact crocodile infested. Today, instead, the Draa after struggling to carve out its route for about 40 kilometres between the Anti Atlas and Jebel Sargho flows languidly for 250 kilometres in a green valley dotted with oases and ksour. Then, at Mhamid, the river course disappears into the sands. Only during some particularly rainy years do its waters manage to reach the ocean.

Tamegroute

Not far from Zagora – a real "gateway to the desert" leading south – the splendid library of Tamegroute is well worth a serious visit. This small settlement is surrounded by a lush palm grove and the many mosques with roofs of blue-green tiles are evidence of its historic, and contemporary, religious role. In the 17th century a *zaouia* was founded here, a traditional religious school that also functions as a sanctuary housing the body of a *marabout*, a holy man who attracts pilgrims. Buried here is Sidi Mohamed Benaceur, founder of the *zaouia* - one of the most important in Saharan Morocco. Thus within the austere crenellated external walls there is an important library that conserves, among the thousands of items held, books written on gazelle hide, ancient volumes of history and medicine, as well as rare copies of the Koran, magnificently illuminated, including one dating from the 13th century.

Old rural houses and busy little workshops situated just outside the town – Tamegroute is home to able craftsmen, particularly skilled in producing ceramics.

Talking of colours

Tamegroute is justifiably proud of its production of ceramics coloured with dyes made from minerals mined near to the town. The busy workshops of these unsophisticated artists are just on the edge of the village. The palette of the craftsman potter is made up of four basic colours: blue, yellow, green and brown. Decorating a white background, these colours are obtained from metal oxides: cobalt for blue, chromium for yellow, copper for green and manganese for black and brown.

Older ceramics can be dated approximately by examining the tone of the blue colour. A bright blue, for example, dates the item from 1881, while a paler shade places it earlier than 1853.

The colourful ceramics made in Tamegroute, noted for the bright assortment of colours and shades ranging from yellow to blue and green to brown.

دكان القصبة
BOUTIQUE LAKASBAH

CAFE DU SUD

Some views of Zagora, a veritable gateway to the desert located some 52 days dromedary ride from Timbuktu, as indicated on a famous signpost (above).

Zagora

As is indicated by a historic signpost, at some 52 days journey from Timbuktu on the back of a dromedary, is a splendid oasis surrounding a town that, while now offering tourist services and structures of a good standard, is still proud of its long and noble history. The presence of piles of stones representing the remains of ancient tombs scattered throughout the valley indicates that the area was already inhabited in very early times. It was in 1056 however, that Almoravide Abu Bakr (who would found the city of Marrakesh eight years later) began the construction of a fortress here that later became the departure point for the ultimate conquest of power in Morocco. In fact, in the 16th century the Saadians, natives of this region, began the conquest first of Souss and then of the whole country at the time under the rule of the Merinid before undertaking the great advance that took them as far as Timbuktu. Today the city, lying 5 kilometres to the north of Jebel Zagora on the banks of the Draa wadi, is the last stopping point before venturing into the heart of the desert. From here the outline of the dunes is visible only a few kilometres away and the desert sands engulf the last trickle of the river Draa. The best way to enjoy the truly splendid panorama is to climb the slopes of the grandiose and lonely rocky pinnacle of Jebel Zagora and admire, as far as the eye can see, the Draa Valley with its palm groves and vast sandy stretches lying between bleak rocky crags including the characteristic isolated mass of Jebel Sargho.

Probably every tourist that has ever visited Zagora has had a photo taken standing below this historic signpost indicating that the distance from here to Timbuktu is 52 days. In the collective conscience Timbuktu symbolises the infinite, it evokes mystery and adventure, it is the glistening city of gold mines (in 1342 the ruler of the city travelled to Mecca with over 8000 bearers and hundreds of camels carrying two and a half tons of gold) that has become a myth, the ultimate goal for travellers. An old Arab proverb states that, "Salt comes from the north, money from the land of the white man, the word of God and wisdom come from Timbuktu." And with good reason Bruce Chatwin said there are two Timbuktus – the real and the imaginary. The metal sign pointing in the direction of a immense void really does seem to suggest that 52 days of travel on camel back will take you to this legendary town. From here on, the notion of kilometres has no meaning at all.

The oasis and the date palms

Whether in the midst of an arid landscape or at the foot of a rocky mountain, the oasis is a symbol of luxuriant nature, of its strength and perennial growth. A synonym for quiet calm, shade and tranquility, the presence of an oasis shows that water is never completely absent in the desert, but somewhere, far below the surface, is a waterbed that allows vegetation to grow above. In fact, a tiny percentage of rainwater infiltrates the earth and reaches a layer of porous rock. Where the water bed is not blocked by impermeable rock then the effect of hydrostatic pressure pushs the water to the surface. In other cases the effect of erosion on the earth lowers the level to such an extent that the phreatic stratum appears on the surface. Thus the oasis, characterised by the slender silouette of date palms, develops like a corner of paradise that can be cultivated and sustain human life. The date palm is considered one of the oldest species of fruit trees in Morocco and is one of the principle sources of sustenance for the inhabitants of the African Sahara and the Middle East.
Over a century ago, the immense areas under cultivation put Morocco in third place in the world for

date production. Part of this was also exported, especially to the English market where the quality of the Majhoul and Boufeggouss varieties is much appreciated.

The date palm is constantly irrigated in the oasis and favours the cultivation of other plants, such as citrus fruits, vegetables and olive trees, by protecting them from the strength of the sun. Pollination of the palm tree is done manually, as in every plot of palms there is only one male for every 50 to 100 females. The operation involves climbing to the top of the palm, which is sometimes 10 metres high, to insert the flowers taken from the male tree into the bunches of female flowers.

Curry

Cardamom

Fennel

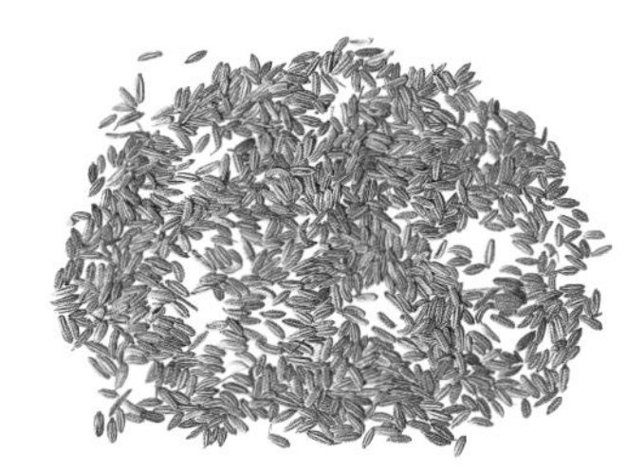

Among the many colours reminiscent of Morocco and its traditions perhaps the most outstanding are those of the rare and highly aromatic spices from saffron to cinnamon, from sesame to cumin, from aniseed to paprika, fennel to curry. These main ingredients of local cookery, displayed in attractive bowls, enliven markets all over the country with their colours. Moroccan cookery is the product of ancient traditions and lengthy preparation and consists of flavoursome, but not too spicy dishes. The spices are, in fact, skilfully balanced in flavouring meat, fish and rice to most harmonious effect and impeccably complement their flavour. They are even used in the sweetest of sweets!

White sesame

DESERT ARCHITECTURE: THE CASBAH AND THE KSOUR

Perfectly in harmony with the natural surroundings, Berber architecture is quite unusual. The casbah and the ksour (plural of ksar) form part of this architecture. The casbah is the ancient residence of the owners who controlled access to the oases, and was built to defend local populations against incursions by raiders. Scattered throughout this region, the casbahs are the equivalent of medieval fortresses in Europe. They have thick walls with corner towers that are castellated. The ground level was used for stabling and grain was stored on the next floor; above this were the living quarters and, at the top, the roof terrace.
The reddish or ochre-coloured towers of the ksour soar above the green expanse of the palm groves, their thick walls pierced by small windows framed with white. These are the fortified villages of the oases, used as communal store-houses and, in times of war, serving as defensive posts. Inside the walls are the *tighermatine*, the fortified houses of wealthier farmers, and the *agadir*, the grainstores.
The materials used are entirely local and all the structures are built with the technique known as 'pisé' – clay pressed together with pebbles and straw – and roofs made of reed matting inserted into wooden frames.

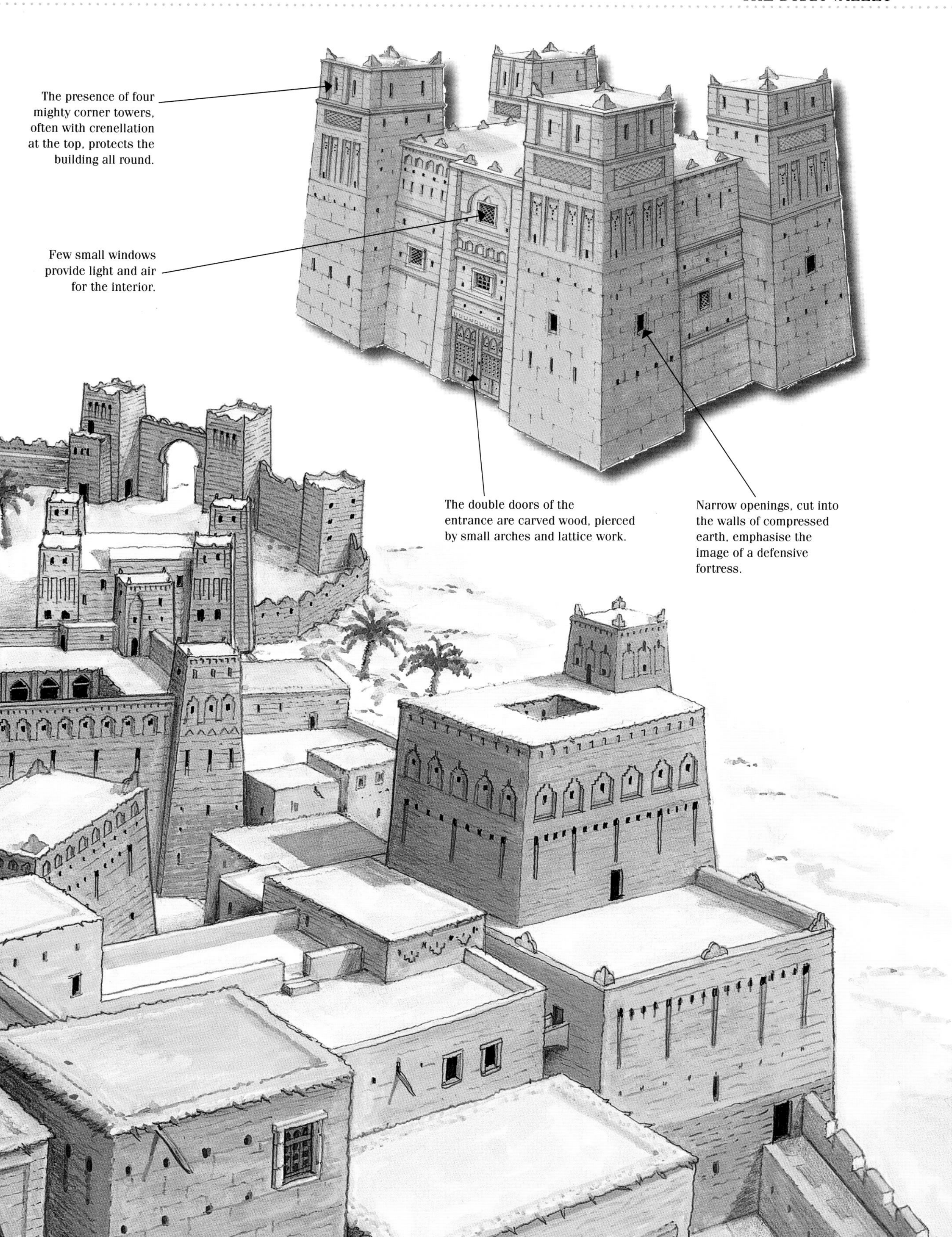
The presence of four mighty corner towers, often with crenellation at the top, protects the building all round.
Few small windows provide light and air for the interior.
The double doors of the entrance are carved wood, pierced by small arches and lattice work.
Narrow openings, cut into the walls of compressed earth, emphasise the image of a defensive fortress.

Following the route of the Dadès, a delightful valley extends between the harsh mountain landscape and deep rocky gorges dug out of the southern sides of the Atlas by perennial wadis (essential arteries giving life to the oases) until it reaches the first dunes of the Sahara. A broad artificial basin has been created by the building of the el Mansour dam, making it possible today to provide regular irrigation for the land in this area, thus facilitating a considerable improvement in agricultural production.
Beyond this basin begins that section of the Dadès Valley known as the "Casbah Route" as it is quite literally dotted haphazardly with splendid oases and consequently with ancient fortified settlements. From Skoura to Boumalne this is the constant and characteristic architectural element of the landscape. And the unique dusky colour of the beaten earth used in the construction of these buildings stands out imperiously against the deep green of the valley, the bright ochre of the desert and the dark, almost reddish outline of the mountains, frequently illuminated by the glistening white peaks.

Skoura

Not far from the el Mansour dam, 35 kilometres to the east of Ouarzazate, in the Dadès Valley is the lush oasis of Skoura an ancient ksar most probably founded in the 12th century by Yacoub el-Mansour.
The name is derived from the Haskoureni, a Berber population who originally settled here, and the settlement is famous for rose cultivation which is surprisingly widespread in this area.
However, the secret of the charm of this town is also certainly due to the splendid oasis, which is not only unusually dense, but also extremely large, sustaining, amidst the green palm groves, a considerable number of attractive villages and impressive casbahs, often exceptionally well-preserved.
Without doubt one of the most majestic and elegant of these is the casbah of Amerhidil, once an important fortified residence of the most powerful family in the region, guardians and lords of the surrounding lands and villages.

Views of the magnificent Amerhidil casbah in the extensive oasis of Skoura.

El Kelâa M'Gouna and the "Valley of Roses"

It might seem strange, but right here in the heart of the desert is the "Valley of Roses", its capital being the fortified village of El Kelâa M'Gouna, high up overlooking the left bank of the M'Goun wadi in the centre of a typical cold oasis. Situated at a height of 1476 metres, the altitude is too great for palm trees to survive but almonds, apricots and pomegranates can tolerate the colder heights. And here splendid rose bushes flourish everywhere along the valley of the M'Goun that becomes increasingly narrow ending in a tapering gorge. Solidly set in a canyon here is the mighty ksar of Bou Thrarar. Much prettier, though, is the environment around El Kelâa M'Gouna where the roses grow and where in the month of May every year a magnificent celebration is held. In contrast, not far from here the village of Azlag is famous for the crafts manufacture of daggers which involves almost its entire population.

From the cold oasis of El Kelâa M'Gouna there is a 360° panorama stretching from the immense valley across to the distant mountains with their snowy peaks. Following pages, stupendous views from a spell-bound world of rocks.

THE ROSE FESTIVAL

Thus every year, for three days in the second week of May, the life of El Kelâa M'Gouna is pleasantly upset by a series of dances and processions that take place beneath a continual shower of petals. For the occasion the residents of the neighbouring villages, splendidly attired in their traditional costumes and jewels, and many young Berber women arrive in the fortified village to participate in the joyous dancing and singing. The festival is one of the most important events of the year, celebrating the gathering of the rose petals. Every aspect of the occasion in El Kelâa M'Gouna is entirely based on roses, from the delicate perfume that drifts on the air to the brightly-coloured petals that float everywhere. The hundreds of people who traditionally spend the month of April gathering about 6000 tons of flowers celebrate the completion of such an immense task by profusely scattering around the petals and rose water. And indeed, the result of so much work is to distill the roses to extract their precious essence.

Spectacular Berber celebrations during the annual Rose Festival.

Produits
Des
Roses
الـــورود
منتوجات

The highland rose

According to tradition some Berber pilgrims visiting Mecca were so fascinated by the beauty and heady perfume of the Damask Rose – the splendid "rose of Damascus" that they decided to bring some samples of this splendid plant back to their desert homeland. Thus began the successful production of El Kelâa M'Gouna and the distilleries that can be seen just on the edge of the town. Due to the abundant harvest of petals carried out mainly by women and children, every year these factories use tons and tons of flowers in the lengthy process of distillation that extracts the precious essence used to produce rose water. It is calculated that more than 7 kilos of flowers are necessary to produce a litre of rose water. As well as possessing numerous virtues and having a highly respectable market value, is also used in many different ways here – in wax and in perfumes, as well as in the products of pharmaceutical laboratories – and is also well suited for export. Indeed it is no exaggeration to state that it provides an absolutely vital contribution to the economy of this region. What are the history and characteristics of this legendary multi-petalled Damask Rose, bright pink in colour and with an unmistakable perfume, that every year in April – and only in April – transforms the desert into a rose-coloured carpet? In fact, this area, situated at quite a considerable height, has a climate that is particularly well-suited to this plant whose origins are still quite mysterious. Some traditions maintain that it derives from India, others that it arrived from the Balkans, imported into Arabia by the Ottomans. Certainly, its flowering is particularly short-lived and so time cannot be lost in collecting the petals. The harvest begins at dawn every day and ends in the early morning in a veritable cloud of the fragrant perfume of these precious flowers.

Although verdant and fertile in places, the age-old fascination of Boumalne du Dadès, dominated by an impressive casbah, is due to its wild, natural setting, typical of rocky highlands.

Boumalne du Dadès

Lying immediately beneath the harsh and dramatic landscape of the Dadès Gorge and overlooking the green banks of the wadi, one of the main attractions of the town of Boumalne is in fact this unusual and extreme environmental setting where the palm trees are unable to grow. In addition to several impressive casbahs, a picturesque weekly market is held in the town. The famous casbah of Tizzarouine, a characteristic structure built in pisé, provides a truly magnificent panorama over this extraordinary region. Also worth visiting is the nearby "Valley of Birds", a spectacular combination of rocky desert plains and grassy expanses fed by the waters of the wadi, where hundreds of birds belonging to numerous species can be seen.

Rugged, inhospitable and inaccessible, the scenery of the Dadès Gorge is one of unique natural beauty where man has, however, managed to establish small, fortified settlements.

THE ROCKY GORGES

The dramatic scenery of the rocky universe that flanks the entire length of the Dadès Valley consists of deep gorges, casbahs perched on mountain tops and craggy precipices where once the fearsome Atlas lion roamed, a feline that became extinct in 1905. The area is certainly more calm and peaceful today as can be seen by the large population of small mouflon sheep, but is, however, still difficult to travel through given the extreme ruggedness of the few pathways. But the views that the Dadès Gorge offers fully justify the discomfort of the journey. It has taken thousands of years of erosion to form the rock and to produce its present colour. Moreover, the vertical walls of the gorge provoke admiration and wonder while even the colour of the rocks amazes, ranging from red to lilac.

Visitors can admire stupendous, sweeping panoramas amidst the majestic gorges of Dadès. At Tmanal, in particular, a series of pink-ochre coloured rocks have soft, rounded forms reminiscent of the shape of feet with gigantic toes. This extraordinary structure has given rise to the area's unusual name of the "Valley of Human Bodies".

CAFE
STAURANT

مخادع هاتفية
ELEBOUTIQUE
هاتف عمومي
أوقات العمل - من 7 صباحا الى 11 ليلا
NESCAFÉ
تلفون

MOUNTAIN ARCHITECTURE

The main type of habitation in the oases and valleys consists of fortified structures, the architectural style of which is derived from many very different influences, especially eastern and pre-Islamic Mediterranean. Most of the casbahs are built on precipitous heights creating an imperious sense of isolation. They are all built in the same style and design and only the various ornamental brickwork patterns differ from one to the other. This decoration is not sophisticated but is dictated simply by the size of the building. In fact, once the construction reaches a certain height, it is difficult to use the normal pisé due to the weight of the wet earth which constitutes the basis of this building material. The walls are therefore finished with pre-dried bricks that are easier to transport. But even here it can be seen that the proud solitude of these places, so strongly rooted in their traditions, has felt the impact of modernity. Indeed, here and there, small bars, telephones and occasional power lines have appeared.

Austere Tinerhir stands beside its palm grove.

Pages 66-67: located amidst the Dadès Gorges, the spectacular Aït Arbi casbah is built of pisé, thus harmonising perfectly with the surrounding environment.

Tinerhir

Situated between the Tafilalet river and the Draa Valley, Tinerhir is a real architectural and environmental treasure. Built in terraces at the foot of a lush palm grove over which the windows of the earth-built houses open, this is a delightful town to visit both for the architecture and the local people. The casbah dominates the houses, palm grove and surrounding countryside. The picturesque and crowded weekly market is held on Mondays – a festive and lively occasion providing a chance to admire the attractive local crafts items displayed for sale. The Todghra Gorge is about 15 kilometres away and many small villages are situated along the course of the wadi, notable for the singular design of the houses. The walls are completely blind and light enters via an internal courtyard which has various functions. This is an ancient architectural arrangement intended to provide shelter from inclement weather and from the heat of the summer, and at the same time protects the privacy of family life from the curiosity of outsiders.

Majestic and spectacular, the Todghra Gorge form an incredible rocky landscape where a dramatic furrow cuts deeply into the heart of soaring rock walls that tower steeply above the visitor.

The Todghra Gorge

The barren and majestic Todghra Gorge is set amidst spectacular and fantastic scenery. The rugged, rocky walls that rise almost perpendicular to flank the bed of the gorge for over 100 metres, reach a height of 300 metres at some points. The Todghra wadi runs through this deep crevice and traditionally the water is used to irrigate fields of almond trees. At the bottom of the rocky walls rises a spring that has always attracted numerous visitors as it is claimed that it has excellent therapeutic properties, especially for women who may be sterile.

THE REGION OF TAFILALET

The region of Tafilalet lies on the south eastern edge of Morocco and was of foremost importance in the history of the country. The Alaouiti dynasty, to which the present king belongs, originated here in 1640. But, for centuries Tafilalet, a main point of access to the Sahara, also represented an important centre for commerce and gold, spices and slaves were transported from here towards Sudan and Guinea. Today it is an excellent tourist centre where the oases blend harmoniously with the dense palm groves and the ksour, numbering over one hundred.

Erfoud

The settlement of Erfoud is situated on the edge of the Tafilalet and the Tizimi palm grove which extends as far as one can see, between the Ziz and Gheris wadis. It was founded in 1917 as a military post and today is the departure point for excursions into the region, and is noted among other things for the date festival which takes place after the harvest, in October.

On the edge of the desert, the recent centre of Erfoud is surrounded by the extensive palm groves of Tafilalet.

ERG CHEBBI

A legend relates that the immense dunes of Erg Chebbi were created by God to punish the inhabitants of the nearby city of Merzouga who had refused hospitality to a woman and her small child during a local festival. God therefore brought about a huge sandstorm that destroyed the village and in its place remained the dunes.
Of all the various forms that the desert can present, that of Erg, although it is only a tenth of the total area of the Sahara, is without doubt the most fascinating. The immense, sandy desert is created by the crumbling of rocks caused by sharp temperature changes between night and day. In turn, the sand, pushed by the strength of the wind, erodes the rocks encountered on its powerful flight.

"The desert is the garden of Allah
from which God
has removed all superfluous
human or animal life,
so that he could have
a place
to walk in peace."

(Arab proverb.)

The Ziz Valley

The Ziz Valley has always been the loveliest attraction in the Tafilalet region. Beautiful and unexpected, this area lies, rich and verdant, amidst the surrounding mountain scenery. The waters of the Ziz wadi flow gently irrigating the fertile banks where luxuriant palm trees grow. Its source is in the High Atlas, as is that of its 'twin' the Gheris, and it comes to an end (again, like the Gheris) amidst the dunes of the immense desert to the south of Rissani, although some legends would seem to indicate, albeit rather improbably, that at least 6000 years ago they acted as tributaries to the river Niger. It is not by chance, in fact, that Tafilalet is described locally as the area where rivers flow to hide themselves before expiring. All around, the contrasting colours of the landscape lend a particularly pleasant and enchanting appearance, emphasised by the presence of the mountain ranges. The chain of the High Atlas – some of the peaks reach over 3000 metres – creates a spectacular natural barrier and

rolls down into the pre-Saharan heights forming semi-arid plateaus at the gateway to the desert. The colour and structure of the ksour dotted around the area blend perfectly with the rocky landscape. The Hassan Addakhil barrage was built between 1968 and 1971 to regulate the flow of the river in order to guarantee the prosperity of the valley and protect it from natural disaster. The barrage forms a lake in this magical countryside which has further improved the tourist attractions of the region, already blessed with considerable resources and amenities, by both nature and man's own efforts. In addition to the overall expanse of this large region, of particular note are the variety of the mountain ranges, climate and people, as well as the range and quality of the local crafts, the numerous historic monuments and sites and the liveliness of the markets and festivals such as the moussem which take place at regular intervals. The infrastructures are also of a high standard: road communications are good and link the towns and villages of the region to one another and to the north of the country. The fresh water requirements are more than adequately met and, with tourism continually and rapidly increasing, the accommodation facilities are of a high level.

Set between the nearby heights, the fertile Ziz Valley, flanking the Ziz wadi, represents one of the loveliest and most popular areas ofTafilalet.

Among other things, Rissani is famous for the great gateway (bottom left), crowned by a green majolica frieze.

Rissani

The road that leads to Rissani crosses an area scattered with ruins, where Sigilmassa stood in ancient times, a transit point for caravans and capital of the kingdom in the 8th century. Today Rissani is an attractive centre with many historic features where a lively market is held three times a week. Nearby stands the mausoleum of Moulay Ali Cherif who was the founder of the Alaouiti dynasty. Destroyed by a flood of the Ziz, it was rebuilt in 1955. The sacred enclosure has a large courtyard which leads to the funerary chamber, decorated with mosaics. Behind the mausoleum lie the ruins of the Oulad Abdelhalim Ksar, the most interesting construction of its kind in the area of Tafilalet.

MERZOUGA: THE DESERT

"The French call the first encounter with the desert 'le baptême de la solitude'. It is a unique sensation and has nothing to do with loneliness, for loneliness presupposes memory. Here in this wholly mineral landscape lighted by stars like flares, even memory disappears; nothing is left but your own breathing and the sound of your heart beating ... For no one who has stayed in the Sahara for awhile is quite the same as when he came."

(Paul Bowles)

Legend relates that one day Allah, enraged by mankind, decided that for punishment he would drop a grain of sand on earth for every sin committed. This was how an area that had before been green and flourishing was transformed into a vast sandy expanse. Thus the Sahara came into being, its name Sah'ra, first mentioned by the Arab writer Ibn Abd-el-Hakem, meaning "emptiness". The word desert (from the Latin meaning "abandoned") is redolent with meaning, emotions, feelings and symbolism. The Sahara is the largest desert in the world, extending in fact over 8 million square kilometres, divided between 11 states.

The history of the Sahara is also that of our planet. Once covered by glaciers, later the sea encroached on the area, albeit partially. At the time of the dinosaurs, it was a boundless verdant plain with rivers flowing and abundant large lakes and swamps. All these climatic changes are indicated by the different kinds of landscape in the Sahara: the stony desert is known as *serir* or *reg* and the smooth pebbles covering the surface are evidence of running water in the past; the rocky desert, or *hamada* was created by the eruption of lava on the surface and, like the stony desert, is criss-crossed by dry riverbeds (wadis); lastly, the sandy desert, known as *erg* consists of large dunes.

The possibility of spending a night in a *riad*, or for the more courageous in a Bedouin tent, should absolutely not be missed. The reward is a black night sky, bright with a carpet of stars, accompanied by the sound of Berber drums rythmically lulling one to sleep.

Discovering unknown Morocco by jeep

One of the most interesting ways of discovering spectacular insights into the real and lesser known Morocco, is to travel into the most impervious areas, least frequented by traditional tourism, in a speedy and intrepid 4-wheel drive that can swiftly transport the visitor on a quite unforgettable journey. In one of these powerful vehicles it is fascinating to discover, on the one hand, the tiny villages that are the gateways and outposts of the immense and inscrutable Sahara, desert of endless solitude. Yet on the other hand, is the pleasure of climbing through woods of cedar and cork trees where there are springs, streams and mountain lakes and, scattered along the slopes of the three ranges of the Atlas, fortified villages are inhabited by Berber populations who have maintained intact their customs and traditions through time. This could, perhaps, be considered an unusual, but certainly a quite fascinating and thorough, way of getting to know the separate and entirely different cultures that have created Morocco. Thus organised expeditions exist for tourists, enabling them to follow a varied route across the entire country from the verdant coastal plains, far up into the mountains, crossing amazing rocky gorges and then descending again to venture into the spectacular sandy dunes of the great deserts. Only the intrepid and powerful jeeps (like modern heirs of the more traditional, but still valid dromedaries)climbing in colourful and picturesque caravans can guarantee to be trustworthy companions on such a demanding journey.

OASIS

THE 'SHIP OF THE DESERT'

The most famous of all desert animals, the dromedary, belongs to the Camelidac family, has a single hump and can be as much as three metres tall. Found throughout northern Africa, he is quite at home in desert areas. Dromedaries eat succulent plants and, when these cannot be found, thorny bushes, and they can even drink salty water without dehydrating. When they have drunk as much as they need, they are capable of resisting ten times longer without water than any other animal, and can thus cross the endless desert for many days without drinking. The hump contains abundant reserves of fat and, as this is consumed by degrees, it gradually becomes softer. Even the unusual form of the dromedary's hooves is adapted to life in the desert. They are divided in two, but joined by a fold of soft skin so that the animal can better distribute its weight without sinking into the sand. And in violent sandstorms the dromedary can even even close its nostrils.

INDEX

The “Blue Men” –

For a long time undisputed masters of the desert were the Tuareg, mythical nomads of Berber origin who constantly travelled the caravan routes of the “bahr belà mà”, the sea without water, seeking cool oases, springs of water and dealing in salt, spices and fabrics, often raiding surrounding villages. It was the Tuareg who commanded and controlled the trans-Saharan commerce.

Today, this ethnic group of fewer than a million people, is threatened with extinction, although they still maintain the customs and habits typical of their nomadic life. The Tuareg are also known as the “Blue Men” as the indaco blue of the robes they wear leaves traces of colour on the skin. The cloak and turban are folded several times to provide greater protection from the heat.

masters of the desert

In Touareg society women are greatly respected and enjoy considerable freedom; traditionally it is held that they imposed the use of turbans, called a "taguelmoust", covering the face and revealing only the eyes, on their husbands, following a battle during which it seems the Tuareg men did not prove to be especially courageous. The nomads of the Sahara call themselves "imohag", meaning "free men". In fact "touareg" is a pejorative term that the Arabs gave them, meaning "abandoned by God".

As for their origins, it is believed that they came from the Yemen, or perhaps are descendants of the ancient Egyptians.

The Tuareg have their own alphabet, known as "tifinar", composed by letters and signs that can be

written from right to left and vice versa: the spoken language is "tamacheq" and it is in this that their stories and legends are handed down.

They are skilled craftsmen and create items and jewellery that are simple but refined. The materials used by the Tuareg to create necklaces and bracelets, earrings and pendents, wallets and bags, are leather, silver and copper.

Their symbol is the cross of Agdz which every craftsman decorates and enriches with his own personal geometric motifs. Each Tuareg group has its own cross, a sign that is of great historic and symbolic importance.

Originally, the Agdz cross was oval in shape, surmounted by a ring that bore different objects according to each tribe. The crosses are usually made of silver as it is sacred to Allah (gold is believed to be unlucky), beaten and engraved by hand. The cross known as "'In Gall" is unique, ending in a bead of red glass.